This coloring book for children is the result of my love for art and children's education. Each illustration was carefully conceived to spark imagination and provide moments of joy and learning. I am confident that these drawings will create precious memories of each child's childhood who ventures into the pages of this book.

Binho Ferrer

2024

This Book Belongs to:

Test Color Page

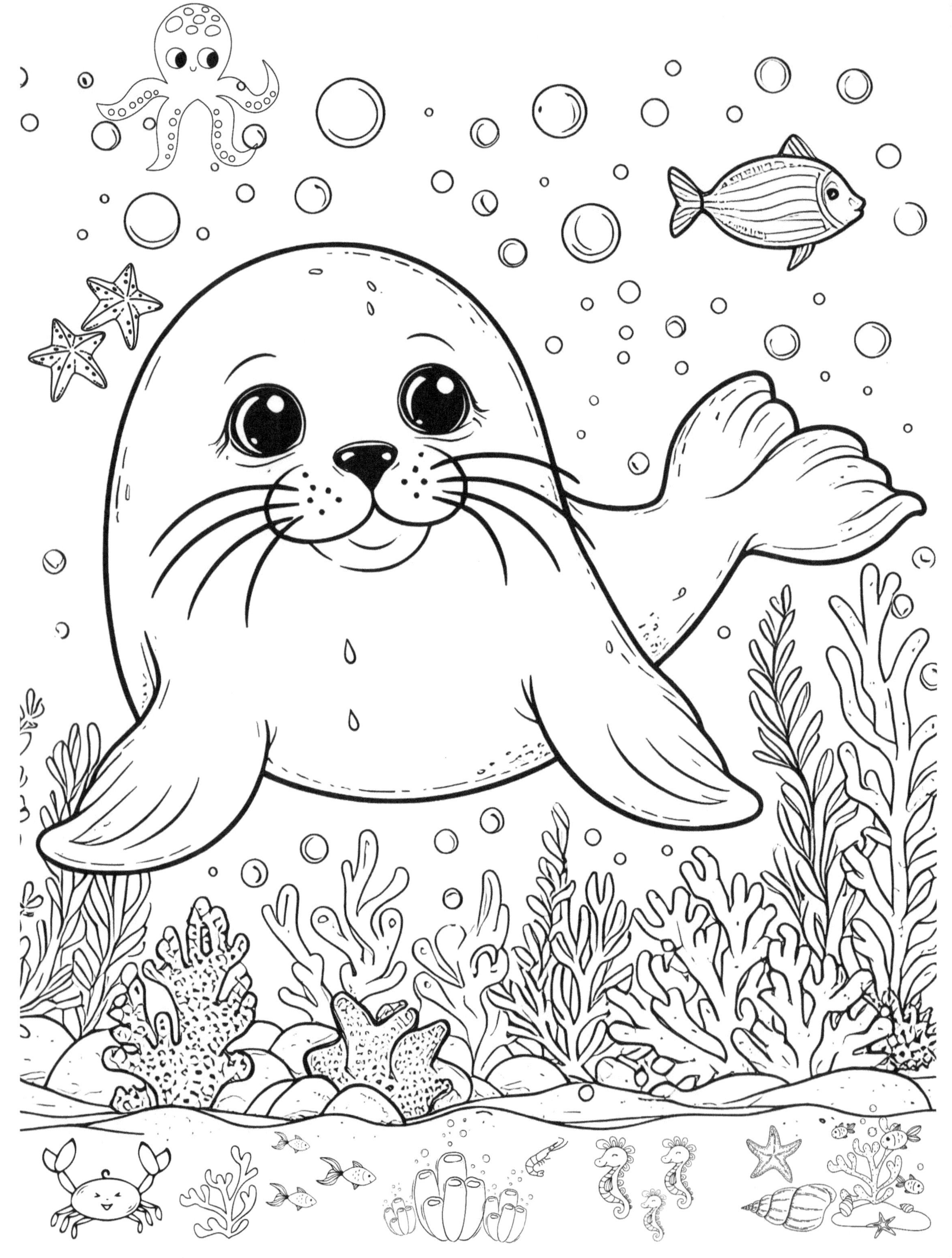